Tourist

Also by Sanford Fraser

14th Street
The New School Chapbook Series, 1995

Among Strangers I've Known All My Life/
Parmi Les Etrangers Que J'ai Connus Toute Ma Vie
Bilingual edition: Tarabuste Editions, 2007, France

Tourist

Sanford Fraser

The New York Quarterly Foundation, Inc.
New York, New York

NYQ Books™ is an imprint of The New York Quarterly Foundation, Inc.

The New York Quarterly Foundation, Inc.
P. O. Box 2015
Old Chelsea Station
New York, NY 10113

www.nyqbooks.org

Copyright © 2009 by Sanford Fraser

All rights reserved. No part of this book may be used or reproduced in any manner whatsoever without written permission of the author. This book is a work of fiction. Any references to historical events, real people or real locales are used fictitiously. Other names, characters, places, and incidents are products of the author's imagination, and any resemblance to actual events or locales or persons, living or dead, is entirely coincidental.

First Edition

Set in New Baskerville

Layout by Raymond P. Hammond
Cover Design by Bob Cooley
Cover Photo: © 2009 Bob Cooley - www.bobcooleyphoto.com

Library of Congress Control Number: 2009932358

ISBN: 978-1-935520-11-5

Tourist

Acknowledgement

My grateful acknowledgement to the editors of the following journals in which poems appearing in this volume were originally published:

Amherst Review
Chronogram
HazMat
The New York Quarterly
The Pittsburgh Quarterly
Wind

I wish to express my appreciation here for the support and suggestions of Christian Garaud, Dorothea Scher, and Angelo Verga.

Contents

I STRANGERS

Tourist	13
Wordless	14
Plymouth Rock	15
Invisible men	16
Homecoming	17
They	18
The House Next Door	19
Number 4	20
Isabel in crutches swings	21
Passersby	22
Old Sylvia, Age Ten	23
Blue Hair	24
Shopping Bag Lady	25
The menu hasn't changed	26
Voices	27
Well-adjusted	28
Faucet Man	29
My Wall	30

II ROLES

In the Land of Fear	33
The TV	34
Don't ever grow up	35
Outfielder	36
John Wayne	37
Sunoco Kid	38
Hanging Out	39

O Say Can You See	40
High Command	41
Puppet	42
Kindergarten Lesson	43
Biker	44
At The Poetry Reading	45
Bus Boy	46
As Usual	47
In front of the waitress	48
Recipe	49
Blue Champagne	50
Any moment now	51

III CONNECTIONS

Love Song	55
When Summer Comes	56
Glimpses	57
Still	58
The way things hold onto you	59
You Never Leave	60
On the subway	61
Clouds	62
Surfer	63
Elevated	64
Light Transport	65
From the airshaft	66
Cages	67
Barnum Dream	68
The leaves are beautiful	69
Frozen	70
At my desk	71
Almost forgotten	72
Almost	73

I STRANGERS

Flabby, bald, lobotomized, he drifted in a sheepish calm, where no agonizing reappraisal jarred his concentration on the electric chair—hanging like an oasis in his air of lost connections....

      Robert Lowell
      (from "Memories of West Street and Lepke")

Tourist

My head,
prayer-bent over a folded map

my eyes, walking
lines

of streets
I don't have time to see

I look up
somewhere lost

among
strangers

I've known
all my life.

Wordless

For a moment
the world is a blank piece of paper

your street has no sign
your building, no number

even the sidewalk and trees
have lost their names.

And the flowers?
The flowers no longer speak Latin.

For a moment
there are no judgments, no types, no titles

everyone you know
is a stranger

unlabeled
free

free for a moment.

Plymouth Rock

Older than the natives
it is slowly stolen

by pilgrims in buses
trains and SUVs

chips of it taken
to distant suburbs

to mantles
above cozy fires crackling,

crackling far from the sound
of cold waves breaking

of ships arriving

chips of history
somewhere dry

among shells
from other shores.

Invisible men

men so familiar
you don't see them on the corner.

Only the strange-quick-spicy sound of their voices
reaches you.

You shut them out
your arm raised for a cab.

A pickup truck slams on its brakes.
Their voices, louder now, chime into you.

For an instant
you see their faces.

Homecoming

Your father and mother
your wife and child
the child you've never seen
in front of you.

Everyone quiet
like strangers
posing for a photograph
their eyes on you.

Your hair, crew cut
your uniform pressed and spotless
a rack of ribbons on your chest
your right arm missing

you take their picture.

They

They march in single file
along the fashion highway

super-thin models
their faces frozen.

For awhile, you're up there
with them

detached

your hips bouncing to the hip-hop beat
your eyes shouting to the applause

Look at me.
Don't look at me.

Completely invisible
in the latest style.

The House Next Door

The PLEASE KEEP OFF THE GRASS sign
stands firm in the front yard
a flat plot of green outlined by a picket fence
for passersby.

The house always seems fresh-painted white.
Behind its drawn drapes, children smile
in jaundiced photographs framed under glass.
A plastic cover guards the living room couch.
Star-shaped doilies shield the Morris chairs.
A child's shoe never wrinkles the azure rug.
The grandfather clock never ticks.

In the garage, a radio plays notes
around the walls. A pinup girl
smiles "Come on" to the Studebaker
stuck in grease.

Number 4

and Julia's husband, you've heard?
Dead near the Bleecker café where I lost my purse
Manhattan toppling over in his eyes without warning
on the way to his car.

He's number 4 in my building this year.
I'm sure you know him well
a quiet man
the flag sewn on his shoulder.

And Julia, what's her last name?
I must send a note.

Isabel in her crutches swings

her extra set of legs, legs polished and veinless
under bulging arms and eyes,
eyes that won't stop seeing
dust and weeds.

In dreams she sweeps the yard
pulls poplars up by their roots.
Her Studebaker starts, then turns
to stone, and she can't move.

Before she wakes, Isabel feels
the crutches inside her fists
the empty sky limping
across her face.

Passersby

Waiting to be waited upon
I watch the passersby.
Some of them remind me
of persons I've known, or know
their legs like the hands of a clock
walking through sunlight,
vanishing.

A tape plays continuously.
I won't remember any of the songs
until I hear them again.

Old Sylvia, Age Ten

Her polite hand raised high
old Sylvia knows where commas go
and she always wins the spelling bee.

The long words walk her past the loud street
where we play Hide & Seek
till after dark.

Home safe behind her book
no one finds Sylvia, slender tall and in her braids
all "excellent conduct" and A's.

Blue hair

cerulean blue
with blond streaks
crossing the street.

She mumbles "I hate you"
her head butting the air
as if someone were there.

Shopping Bag Lady

Tied up inside
the bulging plastic

there's no tree-lined street
in a faded photograph

no voice laughing
in a wrinkled letter

no purse, no ring
only an old woman

on guard.

The menu hasn't changed

she slowly chews her food
he talks to his cell phone

the restaurant, full of loud voices
speaking to someone else.

I'm hungry.

Voices

I keep my eyes fixed
on the pea soup

carefully spooning it
into my mouth.

The voices
from other tables

quickly sink
into its thick liquid.

When the bowl is empty
I use the bread

to sop the them up.

Well adjusted

my watch stares
back at me
the halting step
of its second-hand
silently circling
beneath its monocle.

I lose myself
in its robot movement
till I feel
like a wild animal
wound-up
trapped.

Faucet Man

Someone's touched
the faucet:

it
drips

over &
over again.

I choke it
with a brown paper towel.

Drops of sweat
with their tiny claws

trickle
down my spine

over &
over again.

I pick at skin
below my nails

hold my hand
in scalding water

slowly count to
ten

over &
over again.

My wall

My wall is always there
invisible and in front of me

I feel safe behind it
protected

and of course
locked up.

You're somewhere outside
behind your own wall.

Often, our walls stand together
and talk at each other

their words bouncing
back & forth

not saying much
having a nice time.

II ROLES

Each man in his time plays many parts.

Shakespeare

In the Land of Fear

fear is so small
it can be in a word

or thought

in a nervous laugh
or loud voice.

It can be in small packages
on subway platforms

on your street, on your stoop.

Watch where you step
what you say

in the Land of Fear
snug inside your TV set

is the safest place to be.

The TV

The TV watches me
watching it

follows me
around my mind

around my room
into the street.

Without my knowing it
it gives me a script

what to believe
what to say.

Don't ever grow up

be a Thunderbird boy
all your life

fast, detached and strapped in
behind dark glass and blinding chrome.

Scan suburban lawns for a girl
a poolside girl oiled up just for you

ready to be turned on and
off

or, be that poolside macho girl
your mouth caught

in a mannequin smile
fast, detached, strapped in

driven somewhere else, and
nowhere.

Outfielder

It is always scoreless,
the bottom of the ninth

bases loaded
two strikes, two out.

Naturally, I must play
all positions.

On the mound, I adjust my cap
slowly wind up.

At the plate, I lean forward
squeezing the bat

I pitch. I swing.
Pop-fly to left.

Searching the sky
I run in slow motion, almost dancing

my glove outstretched
a perfect catch.

John Wayne

Half-horse
half-man
on mounted patrol

trapping
me

between the tap
tap
of his iron step.

Sunoco Kid

It's break-time for him:
he kills the Caddy engine
then snaps a Bud open.

When my coin stumbles
through the Coke machine
he laughs

the Lucky Strike
in his mouth
drops out.

Hanging Out

The three of us
drinking Pepsi

Jenny leaning
against the counter

Roger next to her
his hand sliding up &

down her arm
as if he were stroking

a dog
absent-mindedly

no words
spoken

his eyes say
Watch me.

O Say Can You See

My cousin's a pilot in the war.
He sends me pictures of bombs dropping.
At school we bracket verbs and search
for dangling participles. Up there
he cuts the sky and buries bones.

Off Humarock Beach subs are sighted.
The long hands of the sea
so flat and still in the distance
bring K rations to the shore. We raise our arms
like wings and drop stones into the sand.

Each day I walk to the bus stop.
Gloria's there, her breasts already bursting,
her hair too red for Humarock.
My Great Dane Jack paws the dirt
struts his stuff in the morning light.

At school we sing the Star Spangled Banner.
Miss Graham stands while she plays the piano,
pulling the keys like weeds. Old Granite Face
we call her, daughter of the American Revolution
her gray hair and long dress, quiet as stone.

High Command

From posters on the stage
his eyes stare down at us.
Long tubes of light pierce the air
above our heads.
Tall men pace the aisle.
We wait in metal chairs bolted together.

The hallway fills with footsteps.
The loudspeaker crackles.
We stand and mumble the national anthem.
He enters and marches to the stage:
voices cheer, cameras flash
hands rise.

His eyes stare down at me.
He smiles; he laughs. I smile; I laugh.
His mouth opens and his words pierce the air
above my head.
I'm so happy, spit leaps from my mouth.
My hands clap till they sting.

Puppet

He whispers a threat.
I growl and shout it out.

He says we're going to war.
Words march out of my mouth

like wooden soldiers
on parade.

Between acts

I don't know who I am.
I don't know what to say.

Kindergarten Lesson

In narrow lines on pale newsprint
Miss Harper draws her clean and leafless tree.
"Hold the brush like this. Don't drip!"
her voice broadcasts above the little chairs
and button eyes of teddy bears.

The children try to copy her
but soon soft, juicy apples spot and swell
the bending arms of their green trees
as round clouds race to fill the paper skies
before Miss Harper marks
with gold or copper stars

before her bell clangs
"Stop! Clean up this slop
fold your hands on your desktop.

Biker

On my orange motorcycle
the size of my hand

I skip & screech
hard rubber wheels

over the hills and waves
on your front hedge:

hear me *roar, roar
roar* down your road.

At The Poetry Reading

At the poetry reading
you study each poet

your face motionless

as if you were reading a book
a very dull book.

You never applaud.

When you're on stage you seem to toss
someone else's words around your head

your arms waving just so

catching them with apparent ease
like soft rubber balls.

"Look at me. Look at me," your eyes shout.

I wait. I wait for you
to bounce away.

It's my turn, now.

Bus Boy

She doesn't waste any words
on me :

she simply nods her head
and waves her hand
over the saucer.

Oh, I'm sorry
very sorry, I repeat
as if it were my fault.

With my rag I sweep her wine glass
off the table.

Her husband looks up
from his subway map.

There are bits of glass
everywhere.

Do you think the trains are safe, Honey?
...Well, how else are we going to get there?

I want to pour the onion soup
over both of them.

Oh, I'm sorry
very sorry
I'll repeat.

As usual

I wait for you below the glass candles.
The waitress moves slowly
almost waltzing from table to table.
As usual I order moonlight
for the nude beside me
and the waitress laughs as usual.

The nude's in a painting
above a price card
on the cork-covered wall.
She also waits by a window
her eyes searching a moonless night.

A film of varnish guards the ochre skin
of her flat body.
Near her shoulder a titanium sail
bends across a bay
as if reaching out for her.

Finally you're here in the fat booth
beneath acoustic tile.
I say, You're late.
You order beer
the waitress laughs as usual.

In front of the waitress

my father starts pitching
his salesman joke.
Will he ever stop doing this?

We are motionless and silent
waiting for him to finish.
Does he think he's kidding anyone?

Finally, he chuckles
and my mother looks up from her menu :
"The lamb looks good."
"I could eat a horse," he says.

I'm not hungry.
The waitress is wearing a short skirt.
She must think we're all fools.

Recipe

1 Breathy voice
   In a jukebox glow

1 Waiter above us
   With words on tiptoe

2 Rolls in a basket
   Unopened wine

2 Napkins starched & folded
   (1 yours, 1 mine)

2 Faces, polished
   Impasto white

1 Mouth with a grin
1   " drawn tight

Blue Champagne

You're with him
and the band begins to play.

I ask the girl with me.
to dance.

My arm around her
I pull you to me.

Any moment now

Any moment now
I'm going to forget
who I am.

I'm going to disappear
into these words
be someone else

any moment now
maybe.

III CONNECTIONS

Our lives are connected by a thousand invisible threads....

Herman Melville

Love Song

For a moment the sky
is simply up there

just blue
nothing else.

It's not a word in my mouth
or on this page

but blue
just blue.

Not
like anything else

your eyes, for example
not anything like....

Well, maybe
a little bit.

When Summer Comes

When summer comes
in her light sundress
I forget her absence

the walls of my room burst open
the air tastes juicy
acid-sweet.

Glimpses

Glimpses of you
young and shy
suddenly appear

like snapshots
silent and motionless
in my mind.

Here
with taps of my fingers
you're in my arms.

Still

still
in my mind

the water, cold
and waveless

my wet trunks
stuck to me

the towel, grimy
too short for us to lie on

crusts of sand
glued to my back.

I can't remember
what we said

your smile and voice
soft and warm.

The way things hold onto you

The long hands of tunnels, bridges, rails
and streets pointing

away

train-window-hands waving
goodbye

"Yes, I'll write"

your hand at the corner hailing
a cab: "taxi, taxi"

the small hand of its door opening
closing.

You Never Leave

A couple kiss
In the doorway below

Rain chatters on my sill
Thunder snaps in my ear

She stands like you
In that man's arms

Someone coughs next door
A telephone rings

Steps in the hall
Down the stairs

You never leave

On the subway

the laughter of the stranger
beside me
brings back your laughter

your laughter long ago
and now.

Clouds

standing so still
up there

each cloud
a cloud on a blue canvas

here
on paper

clouds
in a word.

Surfer

From the street a child's voice flows
into my room.

I throw the window wide open.
Years fall away:

I'm on a skateboard surfing
high waves roll beneath my feet

seagulls wheel & dive
above my head.

Elevated

above the honking street
the train lifts me
in my gray suit.

Below the track
a biker zooms
through traffic.

My hand twists the throttle.
My elbows cock
like wings in leather.

Light Transport

Its balsa propeller at rest
the model hangs by thread

in the attic vault of air
above my son's head.

I study his craft
like a cautious guest

then smile, remembering
my wish to fly:

the body ribbed taut
in cotton flesh

the wings outstretched
like arms to reach the sun.

From the airshaft

the wild beat
of pigeon wings

breaks in
like a strange voice

high-pitched & dry
almost human.

I want to pin it
down, make it mine

cage it in this space
and time.

Why should I lose it
to the flapping

of wings?

Cages

Each morning the bird seller
stacks his cages on the sidewalk

stacks them high.

Walls of finches tower over him.
Dollar bills flap around his head.

He counts all day.

The tourists keep him in their cameras.
The birds fly off in their song.

Barnum Dream

In my chair the great Gargantua sits.
He's eating grape nut flakes and watching Tarzan
on TV. Tarzan's letting out his god-awful yell
as he swings in diapers over Jane's head.
Gargantua hates Tarzan, and loves Jane.

He's very sad
thinking of the good old days in the circus
the barred room with the hanging Goodyear tire
the desk in the corner, typewriter
unfinished novel.

And the faces
he misses the faces looking in
smiling faces, old and young faces with hands
waving popcorn bags
and red balloons.

He eats a banana and with a sigh
looks out the window.
Animals are still arriving:
elephants honking in the distance
thumping the road, lidding the sky with dust.

I pretend not to notice
he's lost in his Barnum Dream.

The leaves are beautiful

red, yellow, orange
and rust-brown.

I photograph them
bury them in an album.

Red, yellow, orange
and rust brown

they are dying
becoming memories

some of them
still green.

Frozen

a refrigerator by the curb
its door off

a cab inching away
your hand waving.

I want everything
back

the fan humming
the pigeons cooing

the click of steps
in the hall

your voice.

At my desk

my legs are numb as stone
my head, stuffed with words

I stop reading
see myself running at the shore

feel hot sand beneath my feet
cold waves breaking, over my head.

Almost forgotten

the ocean waves coming and going
in the August sun

the steamed clams we ate
around the driftwood fire.

With my toe I draw a curve
in the wet, winter sand.

It's a smile
soon washed away

almost forgotten.

Almost

Through the polite applause
I step onto the stage.

Thank you, I say.
Thank you all for being here.

I can't see anyone:
the overhead light blinds me.

I begin reading.
The character in my poem

sounds like me
and not like me.

Here
and not here

I'm someone else
almost.

photo by Bob Cooley

Sanford Fraser has been a student of painting in Paris and a social worker in New York City where he now lives. He has an A.B. degree in literature from Wesleyan University and a Ph.D. degree in art education from New York University. He has been published in *The New York Quarterly, Barrow Street, Chronogram, The New Laurel Review,* and *Turnstile* among others. His chapbook, *14th Street,* appears in The New School Chapbook Series of 1995. In 2007, his book of poems, *Among Strangers I've Known All Life,* was published in a bilingual edition by Tarabuste Editions in France, where he has also published poems in numerous magazines.

www.sanfordfraser.com

About NYQ Books™

NYQ Books™ was established in 2009 as an imprint of The New York Quarterly Foundation, Inc. Its mission is to augment the *New York Quarterly* poetry magazine by providing an additional venue for poets already published in the magazine. A lifelong dream of NYQ's founding editor, William Packard, NYQ Books™ has been made possible by both growing foundation support and new technology that was not available during William Packard's lifetime. We are proud to present these books to you and hope that you will continue to support The New York Quarterly Foundation, Inc. and our poets and that you will enjoy these other titles from NYQ Books™:

Joanna Crispi	*Soldier in the Grass*
Ted Jonathan	*Bones and Jokes*
Amanda J. Bradley	*Hints and Allegations*
Ira Joe Fisher	*Songs from an Ealier Century*
Kevin Pilkington	*In the Eyes of a Dog*
Fred Yannantuono	*A Boilermaker for the Lady*
Grace Zabriskie	*Poems*
Tony Quagliano	*Language Matters*
Douglas Treem	*Everything So Seriously*

Please visit our website for these and other titles:

www.nyqbooks.org

www.ingramcontent.com/pod-product-compliance
Lightning Source LLC
LaVergne TN
LVHW051850080426
835512LV00018B/3170